AF326565

RESPONSIBILITY OF THE DREAMER

—

JOURNAL

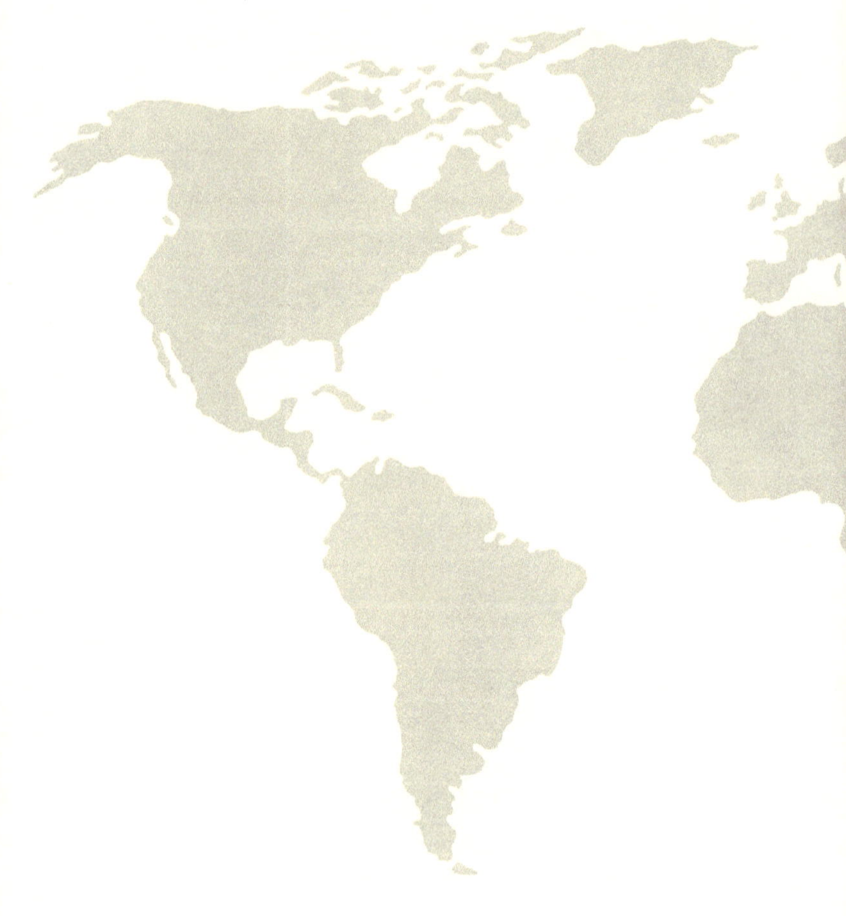
⊙ PLACES I WANT TO GO
✕ PLACES I'VE BEEN
♥ DREAM DESTINATIONS

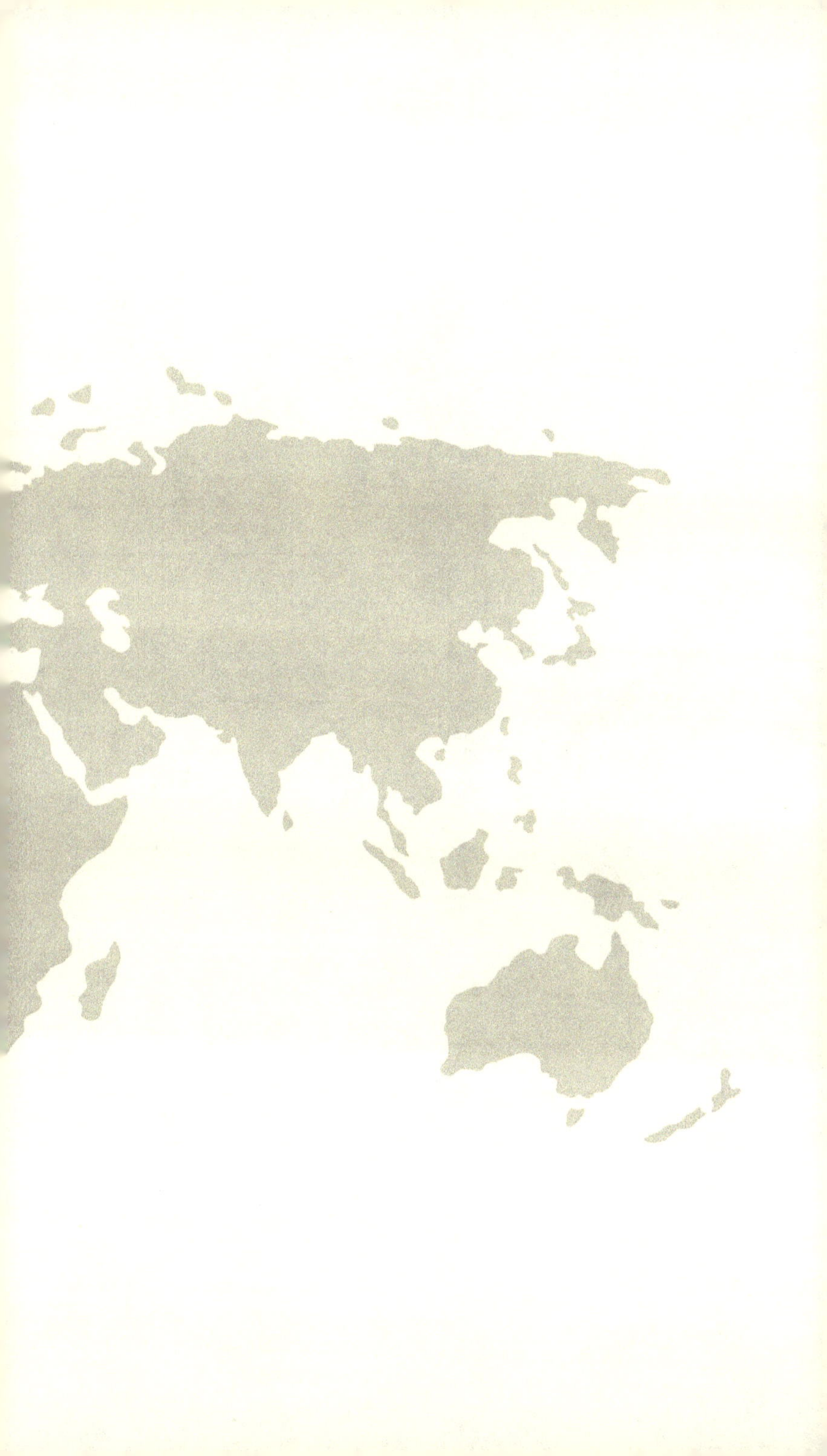

MY GOALS AND AMBITIONS

MON	TUE	WED	THU	FRI	SAT	SUN

MONTH

MON	TUE	WED	THU	FRI	SAT	SUN

MON	TUE	WED	THU	FRI	SAT	SUN

MONTH

MON	TUE	WED	THU	FRI	SAT	SUN

MONTH

MON	TUE	WED	THU	FRI	SAT	SUN

MON	TUE	WED	THU	FRI	SAT	SUN

MONTH

MON	TUE	WED	THU	FRI	SAT	SUN

MONTH

MON	TUE	WED	THU	FRI	SAT	SUN

MON	TUE	WED	THU	FRI	SAT	SUN

MONTH

MON	TUE	WED	THU	FRI	SAT	SUN

MONTH

MON	TUE	WED	THU	FRI	SAT	SUN

MON	TUE	WED	THU	FRI	SAT	SUN

MON	TUE	WED	THU	FRI	SAT	SUN

MON	TUE	WED	THU	FRI	SAT	SUN

MON	TUE	WED	THU	FRI	SAT	SUN

wake easy
rise slow.

DATE   /   /

DATE   /   /

Got to trust that some new love will find its way back back to me

NEW LOVE

DATE   /   /

DATE   /   /

DATE   /   /

DATE   /   /

Be present for
if anything
the memories
that will become
your past
to have something
to look back on

for how sad
it could be
to only have
memories of thoughts
and not thought
of memories

— it feels like a dream

DATE   /   /

DATE   /   /

Quantum fields of loving lost in the times

ADDICTED

I can tell you why
it is important
that we have the ocean
it's the only place
where holding your breath
is better than breathing.

DATE   /   /

And I'm just so grateful that I got to know you here in this universe

I'M WITH YOU

DATE   /   /

DATE   /   /

How do you feel
offline
and is your dream
about how it looks
or how it feels?

— hard questions worth asking

DATE   /   /

Remembering a simpler time of heart and mind

DATE   /   /

DATE   /   /

Don't worry
you're on the right path
otherwise
you wouldn't notice
you were getting off track

remember
life is an adventure
and in all good adventures
somebody gets lost
and luckily
today
it's you!
and not somebody else
lost and amidst
what just might be
an incredible
adventure //

DATE   /   /

I want something I can hold to

Pause
your narration of everything
and let the world around you
speak

DATE   /   /

Life is showing me poetry in motion

DATE   /   /

<u>We are
never here
again.</u>

that's the truth
of our situation

when you consider that
not as a belief
but as a reality

does anything
change?

DATE   /   /

DATE   /   /

DATE   /   /

Of all the steps
choose direction
of all the lovers
choose one
of all emotions
choose love

DATE   /   /

DATE   /   /

DATE   /   /

Thinkin' bout the times when I knew in my heart unconditionally
I could be free maybe we could be free
WHERE DOES THE LOVE GO?

trust

trust

trust

trust

trust

trust

trust

trust

trust

In case you've been forgetting

trust.

DATE   /   /

My heart aches with joy that we call this place home
SINGING FOR COUNTRY

DATE   /   /

DATE   /   /

DATE   /   /

DATE   /   /

Waves
that pass unridden
are not wasted
the only time
waves are wasted
are the ones that are
unappreciated
-

waves like life,
life like waves

DATE   /   /

It's how we turn this water into wine

BLESSINGS

DATE   /   /

Dreams are not like
to do lists
it is not their completion
or reasonableness
that is important
it's the process
of dreaming itself
that much like living
is most enjoyed
unfinished

DATE   /   /

DATE   /   /

Remember you are born of stars you're right just where you are

LEARN YOURSELF

DATE   /   /

The *truly* important things
you do not need to write down
in order to
remember.

DATE   /   /

DATE   /   /

DATE   /   /

DATE   /   /

DATE   /   /

We can live life like adventurers

DATE   /   /

DATE   /   /

The older I get
the more I see
that trying
is neither useful
or productive.

try less
do more

SUN MEMOS • PAGE 83

DATE   /   /

DATE   /   /

I thought of all the distance that's been travelled

FLOWERS BATHED IN SUNLIGHT

Clear your mind
then do the dishes

Better a clear mind
than a clean house
since it's only one of them
we truly tend
to live in

— *Home*

DATE   /   /

DATE   /   /

Can I do the right thing whatever that means by me by you

BLESSINGS

DATE   /   /

DATE   /   /

Thank you
for today
for the challenges
and the easy things
and my chance to enjoy them all
to extend the human spirit
into light

thank you for the health of my loved ones
the meaningfulness of their pursuits
and their ability to see themselves
just as they are

thank you for
the food water air and shelter
that comes from the earth
and thank you for
your natural states
your natural places
your natural sounds
that help me
return
to mine

— *my non-religious prayer*

DATE   /   /

I'm ready now to give my heart to the sea again

DATE   /   /

DATE   /   /

DATE   /   /

DATE   /   /

It's nice
when the wind
knows where it's coming from
and decides to trust
In its direction

— *commitment*

DATE   /   /

DATE   /   /

I'm making space for new love

NEW LOVE

DATE   /   /

Do not seize the day

seize the eve

before the morning comes

floss your teeth

put your phone down

stretch

write

meditate

do what you promised yourself

tonight

so you can enjoy

the morning

and the day

to come

living well is hard

But living poorly

is harder.

DATE   /   /

I could be addicted to you

ADDICTED

*The thing I am most
gravely frightened of
is not experiencing life
As beautifully
as I can express it
in words.*

The loveliest things
you will feel
in this lifetime
are not in words

the loveliest things
are in the writer
and the reader.

DATE   /   /

DATE   /   /

Where does the love go when it's not us?

WHERE DOES THE LOVE GO?